# DEATH & OTHER FORMS OF DEVOTION

Corey Niles

abuddhapress@yahoo.com

ISBN: 9798335590150

*For all those lost to the horrors of silence*

# PART I: INITIATION

### won't you join us

he proclaimed
*no orange water*
*leaking from rusting steel*
*or white concrete*
*pulverized*
*under the heavy tread of man*

he promised
*amber wood*
*emerald grass*
*sapphire water*
*ruby clay*

he asked
*won't you join us*
*in our Garden of Eden*
*don't you want to*
*experience the world through an anointed prism*
*taste the bounty that our king has bestowed upon us*

he whispered
*don't you want to live forever*

**stairway to hell**

I required no railing
or gentle hand to steady
my descent

every turn of that spiraling stairway
decorated with the husks of the hopeful
felt like a distant memory

even if Virgil had appeared
a laurel wreath adorning his head
I would've turned him away

I had witnessed
the devourment of Capocchio's throat
a thousand times

and I welcomed
those familiar circles
right down to the folly of man

**the questions that remain**

was it his starved eyes
devouring me

the black irises reaching out
fork in one hand
knife in the other
preparing for a feast

or was it the golden promises
pouring from his mouth

warm honey
that could crystalize
connecting each hexagonal galaxy
into a universe of possibilities

these are the questions that remain
the desire in his dead eyes or
the beauty of his empty words

**we wed the shadows**

men disappoint
they die
rot

so we wed the shadows
accepted his obsidian rings
took shelter in the night
slept in the cradling arms of darkness

anything could've been waiting for us in that black expanse
enlightenment
damnation

anything

**the disappearing act**

a successful disappearing act
does not require a coffin and chains
or a stage

I merely disrobed
joined the naked bodies
occupying the red leather-clad seats
of your glorious theater

comforted myself in the knowledge that
I was not there to amuse them
I was among the ravenous horde
craving entertainment

**losing each other**

moonshine burned our throats
sugar cubes danced in our heads
and fire flickered in our wide eyes

a reprieve from
a cruel world

the ashes collecting in the bottom of our chalices
reformed into our fallen brethren
and they joined us in dance around the campfire

the only thing worse
than wasting a summer night
was losing each other

**blessed**

we washed the bones
of those unworthy of burial
in his bathwater

we mounted them to
the walls of our sanctuary
honoring his glory
with what was left of them

the murky water
as white as milk
was far purer than
any blasphemous chemical

he'd blessed it with his presence

## something beautiful

he consumed flowers
daisies
lilies
marigolds

ripped the petals off the stems
and ground them to a pulp with
his canines

they never tasted as satisfying as they looked
but for a moment
he had something beautiful inside him

**reborn**

you took my hand
curled it around the top rung of
an electric fence
you held me there
you let the current surge through our bodies
you reminded me
*you're alive*

**help me see**

I was tired of shying away
from sunlight
I wanted to stare into the flames
until it melted my eyes
leaving only charred sockets

I would've rather remembered
the glory
of a few stolen glances at its magnificence
than spent my life
chasing the warmth of its rays

## second mouth

create a second mouth in
my neck
let the blade
allow me to speak your truth
press your megaphone to the wound
so even the onlookers
lingering in the back of the assembly
can hear
how you saved me

## sepia-stained eyes

spring water and self-rolled cigarettes
lazy afternoons on beds of grass
beneath the golden sun

when the day of the week
was no more a concern of ours
than the whims of powerful men and

the blood was colored orange
in our sepia-stained eyes

sun-kissed paint that you slathered
on my bare skin
before promising me
I was loved

**high**

the only time
I ever tasted freedom
was in that dream
all those years ago

I could fly
without the trappings of a plane
I soared through the skies
over houses and highways
wheatfields and forests
scale models of a world that could never have swallowed
me up

and for once
I didn't think about
what would become of my life when I touched down

that's how you made me feel
like I was flying
and all that mattered
was what we did in the sky above

**your eyes**

time melted
butter dripping
liquid gold
down your neck

you ate
feasts
fire
everything before you

and I liked the hunger
the violence
in the dilated black holes
of your eyes

## you moved our bodies

you moved our bodies to
the slowing tempo of my
heart monitor
until my only conception of death was
your thrusting hips
and the burning smell of bleach
filled my nostrils
when you assured me
my last inhalation was that
of pleasure

**butterfly knife**

my body split in half
a butterfly knife of experiences
a black line separating the intricate pattern
of my old life
and my new destiny
a beautiful work of carnage
made in your image

**one of them**

I thought the averted eyes
hushed whispers
were acknowledgments of the change

I was the anointed one
I had been chosen for
another path

I suppose I was right
I was no longer
one of them

**to darkness**

the light pierced my eyelids
red
you brought your hand down over them
returning me to darkness
and I thanked you
for the serenity of deprivation

**strings**

my feet barely touch
the ground as
you move me
to the music

a masterful choreographer
whose strings
chafe my wrists
but whose handiwork
turns my body into
a work of art

there's beauty in inaction
that may have never existed
if the fates cut these binding threads

## la petite mort

I filled your catacombs
with all my little deaths
forced every rigid body into
its final resting place
so others could lay their dying flowers
their fat tears
at your feet
until you
my ravenous incubus
were satisfied

## a wall of blood and unheard pleas

the rocks didn't bounce off her
their trajectory ended
the moment they struck
her flesh

a wall of blood and unheard pleas
for mercy
that I silenced
squeezing the rock harder
and aiming for her mouth

## my mortician

sew my lips into
a smile
and paint them
a rosy red
so they outshine
the pale color
of death

**windchimes**

even after I learned
the windchimes
were made of the bones
of dissenters
I don't think I've ever heard
a more beautiful sound

hollow echoes
that we moved to
when the night wind
rushed through your screen door
and your hands were grasping
my hip bones

**pure oblivion**

there is no better
escape
than exhaustion
don't you agree
aching lungs
pounding skulls
are no more than folktales
when pure oblivion courses through
chapped lips
calloused hands

**paint me**

paint me in crimson
record every imperfection
all my past mistakes and present crimes
in thick acrylic

trap every rotting inch of me in that canvas
then hide it away
so that my likeness
is no more than an afterthought

**your world**

the daffodils
were golden trumpets
that whispered our secrets
in your ears

and the falling rain
anointed you with knowledge
delivered to you alone
from the heavens

and I
I was just another
temptation of the flesh

we all served our purpose
in your world

**watching**

you drew eyes on your purple lids
a warning
even when you were sleeping
you were watching over us
day and night
every hour
minute
second
until we reunite in
your golden castle in the sky

**pose**

take my blood
sink your fangs
into my wrist
drain me
until your cup
runneth over
until my skin
turns to birch bark
and all that is left
is a skeleton
that you may pose
a monument of
my devotion

**your wishes**

the bone of a flightless bird
the streak of light in the night sky
the seeds of a dead dandelion
we reserved these privileges
for our king
you had the power
to make your wishes come true
why waste them on someone
unworthy of dreams

### *good*

we lay on our backs
you stared at the cosmos
I stared at you
you asked me
*why do you avert your gaze*
and I told you
I used to think
the night sky
was full of possibilities
now I know
it's only a reminder
of my insignificance
and you kissed me
and you said
*good*

**devoted**

I wasn't like him
dirt was covering his face
I was holding the shovel
he was merely a blind follower
I was devoted

there was power in sight
a safety

I was sure of it

# PART II: DOUBT

**whole**

the bark ate
the rusting steel
grew around it
before strangling
the dull barbs
becoming one
whole
in death

**waste**

if I was wrong
then every decision
every step
was not a landmark on
my journey to absolution
it was just
a diversion
a mistake
waste

**six-foot holes**

there is a splendor
in a singular purpose
isn't there

an ant
burrowing for its community

there is no question of *one*
among the many
just *us*

but my arms are aching from
digging these six-foot holes for you
my love

**I'm tired of hating Sundays**

the calluses on my knees
have degraded to sores
rosy cheeks
speckled with lemon and plum

and my lips
have dried
split
spreading open like your once welcoming arms
with each word I mutter
to the heavens

I may not be able to walk
from your alter
but I will crawl

**mourning doves**

doves fly
in figure eights over your garden
embodiments
of the Holy Spirit
you tell us

but look closer
at their narrow faces
of singular sight
and blank stares

appreciate the sharp talons
stained in pale patches
from where you bleached
these mourning doves
white

and forget about how
the worms
writhing in their mouths will
never make it to their squabs
after you captured them

**folded in prayer**

why stop at my nails
take my fingers
my hands
sever them
at my wrists
what use are they to me
folded in prayer

## their quiet graves will hear

pronounce your love
upon hilltops
below
their quiet graves will hear
how well you appreciate
all the lost birds of paradise
once they've gone extinct

**choke**

does your cape
ever weigh you down
my hero

does it pull at your neck
press into your throat
as you come to the rescue

more importantly
do you like it

**your prayer**

I chant them
your words
but they have long since lost
their meaning

just part of the act
forcing sound out of my
mouth
to satisfy your whims

only a test for those
who can't remember
the words
that please your ears
or those who are bad at
faking it

**unfocused eyes**

so many unfocused eyes
look favorably upon
you
why do you need mine
to see yourself

## my death

I worked
my body to
ruin

I scattered my past
into space
let it disintegrate
in the atmosphere

I gave you my life
but I can't
won't
give you my death

**did I**

did I suggest
we retire for the night
that first night
or was I
following orders

I remember everything
the sickeningly sweet wine
his acrid sweat
the effort of presenting joy
everything
except for that detail

it won't change anything
but it matters
a reason as elusive
as the smoke that
danced from his cigarette
in that dim room

I suppose
whether or not I saw an opportunity
or I was just being a good soldier
I could no sooner stop the proclivities
of a god
than capture those tendrils of smoke

**mine**

water won't
wash away the oil of
your touch

so I lit a match
burned it away
screamed
until it charred my nerves

and all that remained were
muscles
tendons
veins
bones

mine

**scraps**

your scraps of meat
provide no more than
a fatty distraction

all flavor
no sustenance

I'm hungry
starving and
I'd much rather flip the table
than wait for your inconsequential
generosity

**your demise**

an idea
that's all it was
that I didn't have to
march like your other men
that I had a hand in my fate
a choice
that's what ultimately led to
your demise

**you**

you have no more of a connection to
the old gods
than the texts hidden away in your office
no one is coming after us
there is no grand conspiracy
or paradise waiting for us
on the other side of this hell
you stole the brooch
you took the picture
you saw the flickering lights
it was all you

**we are not the same**

you don your robes
royal purple silk and solid gold
chains
and dead eyes that
drew me in like whirlpools
I'm just a waterlogged body
floating in your red sea

**burn**

I didn't create the spark
I couldn't have known
the way that old wood would ignite
how the stained glass would melt

but I lined the matches
between our kneeling figures
around your pulpit

placed them so precisely that
there was no chance of it
burning out

when it finally caught fire
when their ears grew tired of hearing
your lies
I knew you would burn

and you did
with such magnificent glory
I'm sure even the old gods
could see it from the sky

**I'm sorry**

but I won't lay down with you
in the rubble of something
that never reached
the beauty of its potential

I'd rather live among
the heathens
where happiness is limited but
it's real

# PART III: AFTERMATH

**end of an era**

it was never about her
or her unborn child for that matter
not to us then
and certainly not nowadays

it was about the end of
slathering plaster over
cracked walls
pretending that they'll stand
forever

a stripping away of the façade
revealing the corpses that have
insulated our happy homes
for far too long

**crimson world**

when the walls bled
too much for your precious soil
to soak up your mess
and you took the stage for your
swan song
did you ever question
all that you've done
or did you bask in the crimson world
you created

## goodbye

I didn't walk away
I sawed your
clutching
grasping
outstretched hand
off at the wrist
dunked it in my river of tears
until the flesh peeled off
a glove that I donned
when I waved
goodbye

## I thought of you

I don't know if it was
the sharp February wind
that greeted me at the front door
or the bloated raccoon
I passed on the highway
but today
I thought of you

**you weren't the party**

even when your eyes were
glazed over with poison

you were the late mornings
the pounding headaches
the wonder if
losing yourself to the night
was worth forgetting yourself in the day

you weren't the numbing music
or the endless possibilities of
a Friday night

you were the bloodshot eyes
the immobile bodies
the regret

**I'm alive**

can a drowning man be faulted for
pulling himself out of the water

even when he
drags another man down to
keep himself afloat

even when the air is
far too sweet to hear
his victim's garbled screams
below the surface

even when a part of me enjoyed it
because
you never cared enough to toss me a life raft
so I created my own

I won't apologize for
taking what I needed
I'm alive

**interview**

the sky darkens
before lightning strikes
a rabid dog barks
foams
before he lunges
of course there were warning signs
yellow
black
lining the road
but I only had eyes
for him

**one favorable look**

was it a mere coincidence
that the spell of you
possessed my mind
that the feeling of your lips
annihilated any sense of morality or logic
my parents had instilled in me
I have to believe
it was you
because the reality that
we are all one favorable look away from
providing our lives to a stranger
is too terrifying

**your ghost**

an unexpected knock
on the front door
a stranger's
lingering stare
a truck that remains in my rearview mirror
a little too long
your ghost colors every
uncertainty

**fused**

there is no severing
the monster from your visage
the flesh has molded
the feet of that wandering man you saved
rot and regrowth interwoven in
the very fabric of the black socks he wore

so what am I to do with
the knowledge that you found the indoors suffocating
that you rarely slept through a night without
shouting in your sleep
that you carried a yellowed photo of your mother
when she was young

these I can't amputate from my memory
without the pain that man experienced
eyes shut tight
when you ripped off his socks
and tried to make him whole again
never considering the rot
traveling to his heart

## the sculptor

I won't erect statues
in your honor
you have enough young men
laying flowers at your alter

I'll tell onlookers
that you were once human
glorious
monstrous
beautiful
terrible

a stack of overlapping negatives
that could never be detailed in
a stone as cold as marble
or understood by any man
who shared your bed

especially one
armed with a hammer and chisel
and a penchant for perfection that
only exists in retrospect

**their eyes**

their faces follow me
in stained cigarette butts
crushed beer cans
crinkled aluminum wrappers

in the darkness
the light of my memories
catches in their eyes
as they stare at me in the night

all the offerings
I laid at your feet

**the tapestry**

it's a disease
isn't it

an eternal displacement
trying to track every thread to
see where the pattern changed
or was formed
all the while knowing
the blanket is finished
the creator is dead
and picking it apart
will only destroy it

but when the tapestry
depicts such a hideous scene
does it really matter

**scissors**

I picked them up
set them aside
thought of all the
beautiful ways
I could reattach
the strings
until I remembered
I'm the one holding the scissors

**is there a difference**

offering my throat
at your alter
or starving on these streets
too proud to even
seek shelter
in another person

**in his absence**

unless you've danced with reality
felt the comfort of his arms
wrapped around your waist
and then lost him in the crowd
can you know the fear of
trying to find him
in the labyrinth of moving bodies

and suddenly you are the boy
cheeks flecked with luster dust
placing a heart-shaped tablet on your
tongue

and the man
grinding into his lover
hands moving down his mesh shirt
toward his unbuttoned jeans

and the woman just outside the bar
cigarette in hand
face glowing in the lights
flashing through the cracked windows

and even when you find him again
press your body into his
join him once more on the dance floor
there is still the question of who you were
in his absence

## asleep

I never woke up today
some part of me is stuck
in that bed
in those worlds without reason

a part of me likes it
the volume has been turned down
muted
the world is out of focus
a blur of inconsequential life

but the sharpness
the edge
is gone

a sterling silver butter knife
beautiful in its intricate design
but ultimately
dull

**my first crime**

you told me that
the world moved
rotated
because you pushed it under
your heavy tread

and I
well
my first crime was
believing you

**exist**

keep your diction
and your love of
the classics
I don't want to know the world
I want to be an unenlightened part of it
never questioning whether or not
my thoughts align with Plato
I just want to exist for one moment
a single second
without considering
the implications of each breath

**killing you**

I had a funeral for you
my little friend
laid you out
on a raft
burned your body to ashes
and sent you down the Mississippi River

a few weeks later
I did it again
fire
water
a farewell

over and over again
I don't know if it felt good the first time
if I felt some sort of relief
but now it's just a habit
killing you

## glass coffins

I don't want an apology or
a declaration of all the ways
I was wronged

I know
what you did to me wasn't okay
or fine
or any of the little lies we use to
suffocate in glass coffins

I don't need to forgive you
to pull myself from this ornate box and
get on with my life

**front page**

I saw him today
no straggly hair
or scarred flesh
just a young face
tight smile
eyes only deemed dead
when we discovered
he was staring into an abyss
captured in ink and paper
below a list of his accomplishments

I ripped it to pieces
cast it to the wind
so that if I had the fortune of
forgetting his face
I'd never have to see him again

**tell them**

that I know
it took too long

that the same blinders
nailed into the sides of their skulls
narrowed my vision

that while none of us can ever trust
the weight of words again
I'm sorry

that maybe all we can do is
promise to not forget
those lost to the horrors of silence

that we can swear to catch the ones
nearing the cliff drop
we were lucky enough to
survive

that even as I write these words
I know they serve as a greater comfort
to me

that they are
nevertheless
true

**ruins**

all that remains
of his town are
ruins
stone squares that
once served as the foundation
of his holy cause

will this graveyard
always be tainted by
what he's done

or someday
will someone discover this place
imagine great castles
knights
kings
queens
where decency and loyalty
held more importance than love

something beautiful
that can be built from
all the destruction
we created

**the sun**

I can never look to the sky with hope
when I know the power it can hold
in the wrong hands

but today
the sun came out
skittering between stratus clouds

and for the first time in a long time
it didn't remind me of him
or us
or anything

I appreciated its warmth
however limited and fleeting
and I went about my day

# ACKNOWLEDGMENTS

I started this collection in 2020 during a dark time in my life, and I want to thank the family and friends who were part of this journey from then until now. Thank you for your love, support, and belief in this collection.

First and foremost, I want to thank Sean Lowers, who is my partner in every sense of the word. Thank you for your constant love and encouragement.

Thank you to my fellow writers, Caitlin Hensel, George Galuschak, and Sara Tantlinger. I appreciate your invaluable advice and, more importantly, your friendship.

Thank you to my first poetry professor and mentor, Timons Esaias. Rarely does a day pass without one of your indispensable lessons crossing my mind.

Thank you to my family and friends, including but not limited to, Amber and Patrick Beets, Joe Lewis, Jeffrey J. Niles, Megan Matejcic, and Marisa Balatico.

I owe a special thanks to Alexander, Boo, Andy, Byron, and our found family in Durham.

Last, and certainly not least, I would like to thank Alien Buddha Press for sharing my work with your readers and providing this collection with an amazing home.

Corey Niles is a queer writer and poet from the Rust Belt. His poetry has appeared in Nightmare Magazine, The Literary Hatchet, Chlorophobia: An Eco-Horror Anthology, and the HWA Poetry Showcase. His debut novel, Blood & Dirt, was released by NineStar Press in 2022. His second novel is forthcoming from Crystal Lake Publishing.

Made in the USA
Middletown, DE
26 August 2024